VANISHING POINT

To Susan with Best Wishes from Tony Petch

by Tony Petch

2003

Ragged Raven Press

Snitterfield, Warwickshire

VANISHING POINT

First published in England, 2003 by Ragged Raven Press
I Lodge Farm, Snitterfield, Warwickshire CV37 0LR
email: raggedravenpress@aol.com
website: www.raggedraven.co.uk

Vanishing Point
ISBN 0 9542397 3 3

Set in Arial.

Printed by Lithocraft, 35a Dane Road, Coventry, West Midlands
CV2 4JR

VANISHING POINT

by Tony Petch

2003

To Jenny

And thanks to Andy Fletcher for suggestions regarding many of these poems when they were in draft form.

CONTENTS

Page

ACKNOWLEDGEMENTS

Thanks are due to the editors of the following publications, in which several of the poems in this volume first appeared: *A Rumoured City* (Bloodaxe, ed. Douglas Dunn), *Poetry Review*, *Mutiny Poets*, *iota*, *Stoneferry Review*, *Inkshed*, *To Build a Bridge*, and *Proof* (Lincolnshire and Humberside Arts). Several poems have appeared in the pamphlet *The H.U. Principle* by Stone Creek Press (1992) and the Ragged Raven anthologies *Old Songs Getting Younger*, *Smile the Weird Joy*, *Red Hot Fiesta* and *Saturday Night Desperate*.

Moths

My uncle collected moths.
Moths. Moths. Moths.
The moth Beatrice
peeping at me from behind her skirts.
The moth Sinclair
on his way to Egypt.
Yes, journeys are hard to fasten down.
Directions change the location of places.
Try reading my uncle's trembling script
on the labels in the display case
and you'll discover how the flight of language
settles with tiny hairs.
Try deciphering the words
and you'll see through meaning
to where our voices clog with fluff
and the tongue shrivels.
Underfoot towards autumn
dry leaves have less and less to say.
Time runs out of marriage.
On their wedding night
Lomax and Winton clasped wings.
Look at their youthful presence under glass
where my uncle pinned them,
the haunted eyes of Muriel,
her name in my uncle's writing,
Mrs Usher and a second Lomax also on show.
Who are they? Who were they
and who will they be?
I don't have a moth book
to look up their proper names.
Outside at night
my uncle shone his lamp to attract them.
Running with his net through the darkness
he tripped on a beam of light
and fell as we all do
and now
he's in the display case as well.
What was he called?
There he is.
The wingless one.

On the terrace

We're out on the terrace in the sun.
Claude's painting a picture of houses opposite.
He's squirting blue acrylic into a white plastic tray
adding blobs of yellow and green
before picking up the brush again
to work away towards the bottom of the canvas
on the bit where a creeper is growing close to a low wall.
He says he doesn't mind me watching.
I've always thought it must be lovely to be able to turn scenes
and views
into something that in some way is your own.
Now he's putting in the flaky trunk of a huge London plane tree
that overshadows the terracotta tiles of the old buildings
he's outlined in pencil.
It's the sort of day people like to remember
though times like this are easy to forget
because often there doesn't seem to be much going on.
At my feet Claude's dog is asleep
but her legs are twitching
as she runs to or away from something in a dream.
Above the noise of gulls
a toddler in a pushchair down on the road gurgles
as windows and curtains start to appear in the painting
before the sound of the bristles being swirled again in a jar of
water
after a fresh application of red.
I don't need to be around to see the picture finished.
It's sufficient to feel part of the process just long enough
to experience the changing patterns of the mood and the sky
without knowing where all this will lead
or where any of us may go.

Digging

When a train passed our allotment
my father would stop the row he was digging.
To rest his back he'd count the trucks.

When I dig
sweat from my father's forehead stings my eyes.
I dig down deep in search of my father,
not the father I knew,
the one I came to know less and less
till we only shook hands when we met,
but the father I feel I ought to have had.

I dig beyond my father's allotment.
I dig to where I last saw him.
I dig past death to birth and beyond.
Through shadow, through absence, through thought I dig.

Now I'm a father as well
I dig through myself.
In rain and wind
through flesh and bone I continue.
When trains go by I carry on digging.
I dig past fire, past darkness.
Even the disappearance of space doesn't stop me.
Just for the feel underfoot
I dig into digging.
Just for the feel of the sting from the salt of the earth on my face,
through fathers I know and fathers I don't
I dig.

Blue

My father's in the chair having his head painted blue.
Just before she finishes
the painter picks up the wrong brush.
Now there's a spot of green on my father's ear.
She winks at me.
We're not going to tell him.
He's about to walk out of here
into a busy street
with a spot of green on his ear
and he's not going to know.

Trains

When the rails on the embankment hum
go and look out the window.
Here comes a train. Plenty of steel and coal
down the single track.
Thirty six trucks to the docks.
Always thirty six trucks.
We look up the locomotive's name,
Ogmore Castle.
Turning the page, there's its picture,
loadhaul liveried Class Fifty Six,
number five six zero three four.

And then
one day, on its own,
for no apparent reason,
a shunter from miles up north.
It came down this bit of line
and went back.
A good view of the city up there from the cab
so near our little house,
factories and traffic
through a moving screen of sycamore
with hawthorn in flower.

For no apparent reason
white and green
brighten the busy fumes of the day.

Suddenly one night

It seems odd
that there was no contradiction in the dream –
I knew he was dead
but my father took my hand
and guided it across the paper
as I sat with a sketchbook on my lap
so I could get the perspective of the trees and the mountains
right.

He was good at painting landscapes
and unlike mine
when his colours ran
they were meant to
so maybe I should also mention
the time we were driving in the Highlands.
A storm was passing
and he stopped the car on a hairpin bend
to catch a rainbow.

Another day
when drawing a barn in a field
he put in a stem of hogweed as foreground.

Suddenly one night
my mother felt him leap up from the bed.
He tumbled to the floor.
He didn't move.
She saw his purple face
and knew he'd gone
leaving her alone
with the mysteries of moss and fern and fen
and the youthfulness and birth
in stillness and silence that persists.

Psalm 75 begins
Unto thee O God, do we give thanks,
unto thee do we give thanks:
for that thy name is near thy wondrous works declare.
This is one of many quotes I could have used
for my father who believed
in a way I sometimes wish I did myself.

My parents had gone to stay with friends
the night he died.
They sat up with my mother till the morning.
I don't know if they could see the stars
but I feel we'll never quite understand
what's out there.

The advancement of knowledge

My grandfather kept stars.
Sussex stars. The last of the breed.
They were good layers,
ghost stars giving birth
to ghosts.

When he was hungry
he would wring their necks
somewhere in the nettles.

In the village school
where I learned to count ghosts
and nettle stings on my fingers
is a picture of a chicken –
and a star.

Platform One

I walk along the platform
sit down
and put my luggage beside me.
Suddenly one of my carrier bags
puffs itself up
struts towards a pigeon
picks up a few crumbs on the way.
The young woman on the seat near me
gives me a funny look.
Then my suitcase
stands on end
takes a quick bow
and does a brisk tap-dance in front of us.

These are my belongings.
In these hold-alls and bags
I keep my house
my friends
my food
everything I know.
I've always had this problem
of being on some perpetual journey
my luggage embarrassingly out of control.
I'm never quite sure where I'm going.
The trains that arrive here
are never destined for the town I thought I lived in
the town to which
I'm always trying to return.

Sunflower

I'm turning into a village.
I try to stop myself before I go too far.
Already I'm two houses.
What is to become of me, I wonder.
I daren't go indoors.
I try going to the doctor.
Oh no! Here I am turning into
the main drive up to his surgery.
To stop myself, I get down on all fours.
Stop! Stop! I shout for years I get lost in
which turn into moments of half-truth
like half-eight or twelve midnight,
moments from the twelfth century B.C.
I can occupy darkly
wearing a tweed hood,
its Cro-Magnon centre-fold
flashed with electric blue.
One moment a photograph of it,
the next a chuckle with authentic tosh,
an identikit picture of me
and a tendency to go over the top,
that tendency of the universe
to comprise overlapping gaps
hopping over each other from monument to monument
sandwiched by the double life
of the foolish things in my headgear
like love in Kensington High Street, for example,
or the policing of galactic attraction
in the shunting yard of moments from here to there
by shifting the weight you attach to the importance of each
from the foot of one instant to another
in massive, high risk,
twenty minute
bursts.

Jackey & John

You fall in love, live together
and try to find each other by going to Greek islands.
It's better than all the jewellery on the world's fucked-up fingers.
A little dot on the horizon's a temple three thousand years old.
The bit of B.C. marble you handle is chucked in the sea for
Dionysus.
I couldn't, myself, have eaten Otis the Octopus out there
but back here, at home, over ratatouille, black eye beans in
sauce and pork chops with chips
you tell me how women came down to the beach with spinners
and no bait to catch squid,
how steep it gets when you climb to the caves
that remind me of Conrad's *Heart of Darkness* I've never read,
how the dog that runs the island and knows everything
sticks its nose up the arse of a nude French girl walking into
the waves,
and how, under a stone in a shepherd's hut
you find a book on ancient and modern history.
From the past comes the tittle-tattle of little bones in the tin
in the church with the tiny door you could hardly get through.
Talking of doors
we're now onto the ice-cream we got up the road at Kwiksave
where I felt like showing my passport to the security guy at the
entrance.
It's eight-thirty p.m. in winter at the end of the twentieth century
in Hull.
We raise our glasses and say cheers to the way relationships
gather wrinkles
rather than go in straight lines,
and to the way, when you got the films developed, the colours
didn't come out as you hoped.
That's Jackey's armpit when the automatic went off too soon
and this is a shot of the luggage John kicked the shit out of
when you both got stuck at the airport.
I hopped up and down the hall when you invited me round
tonight.
A wasp I didn't see on the handset
stung my thumb when I picked up the phone.

You thought I screamed with delight
as its tired hairy late-season sea-horse body
top-heavily buzzed around in the air.
With the deep faraway living of people we never meet
sometimes it's hard to tell excitement from pain.
But here's to hoping things last between us
as along with our expectations
we lower our glasses having drunk too much wine.

1903

That fucking spaniel again. Gets everywhere. Was alive in 1903, too.

The bloke on the horse – what's the Dutch for Fred? The oil on the canvas squelches as he starts to move around in the picture. He puts his hand down the front of his trousers and removes a massive codpiece the size of a size thirteen cucumber with which he starts to beat the yelping spaniel about the head for snapping at his horse's heels. *Take that, you bastard!* he screams in Dutch, *And that! And that! And that!* (All again in Dutch).

The racket echoes throughout the gallery. On hearing the rumpus, an attendant in 1903 attendant's uniform comes rushing up to the huge gilt-framed portrait and plunges his fist deep into what, by now, is a sort of 3-D pudding of sloshy oils and yanks the spaniel from the blows of its master's cudgel. *Poor little thing*, says the attendant in English (the gallery being in England). He dries his eyes, and before turning to deposit what by now is a shitty little canine corpse into the litterbin, he takes one almighty kick at the Dutch freak in the frame.

discovering john

discovering john
discovering john ringing
discovering john through history
    through towers and belfries
    and the towers before them
    and before that
    when towers weren't towers

discovering john through the history of ringing
and discovering john withdrawn from bells
    to accidents with odds and ends
    far down the index of ringing
    and beyond sound

discovering john beyond the fortress of government
discovering ourselves
through john
    our names
    and how ignorance rung loudly
    becomes a gargantuan I.Q.

discovering john beyond john
discovering how a bell
can ease the invasion of the sea
to reveal the unknown
    the axle system
    monastic throughout

discovering john through the discovery that light has history
and the discovery of discovery
the removal of john and st. margaret's ringing
    of prestige
    of smoke
    of gold bracelets
    and god

discovering john by ways of beginning
the restoration of john
and all the other queens and saints
these gradual deacons, decoys and wonderful
monsters
we all are

dong

dong

dong

each moment open to find out

Buggy

In the grass at the side of the path on top of the cliff
a child's buggy covered in rust.
You're wondering how it got through streets and fields to here
where we sit.
We look over plantain and stitchwort
to a boat heading out to sea.
Behind us land's slipped.
The track's been re-routed.
The past's in mid-air.
You pick up the buggy and try to unfold it.
It feels like a child could be missing.
Above us
below
and beyond us
there's more.

Going

I remember you
in the distance
of what's left of your smile.

I can't stay with you.
The tide's going out.

I put a match to edge of the day,
see it flare in the evening sky.

In the physics of loss
does flame have mass?
In the mathematics of bereavement
does two minus one equal zero?
In the geography of loneliness
do hills turn away?
Is solitude marked on a map?
In the language of longing
is love no longer a word?

Cards and flowers don't answer questions,
and it's easy to disobey orders like *Get Well Soon*.
Had we a theory of everything
not even that would explain,
since we don't understand all we know.

What I know
amounts to a cargo of feeling.

Where we're blown, fair and equal,
full sail, I see it disturbing the air.
And it's here, at a shoreline, I find myself
watching you go.

Apart

Now I've left
no longer do you have to keep the knives so sharp.
I won't be writing, calling or popping up in your herbaceous
borders.
Lettuce, jewellery, the morning mail,
all undergo your inspection to ensure nothing of mine,
not a freckle, not a frown or ruckle should remain or appear.

Does laughter slip on soap?
Not any more.
Even the hyena's given up on our show.
Broadway's looking for more lustre these days.

Latterly, I was so jumpy
the clothes I was wearing ran ahead of me.
My dirty washing had to be harpooned.

Now I've caught up with all my shirts and trousers
I've time to whistle and throw out my arms
without feeling I should be rolling pastry
or pumping up tyres.

No outfit could have mended the puncture between us,
but out here on my own I can speak Italian badly,
and if I want, use my fingers to eat sausages
even if it's not done in Rome.

Not any more are spots of fat on my tie open to scrutiny
and my sentences can be as long and as muddled as I wish.
I can take out a loan on a bunch of carnations
or, to add to the millions of bits of information that litter the
untidy mind,
look up the definition of carbide before the end of the quiz.
Since I've gone, friends can't help noticing how white your
sheets have become.
No longer are you afraid to hang them in the garden to dry.
Were we to write to one another
how clean both sides of the paper would be.

Doorstop

We're splitting up.
I stack books ready to move out.
In the sunlight through the door propped open by an iron cat
dust dances.
On the shelves
it's thick enough for me to write our names in.
As I start to pack a cardboard box
I push back the flaps
sensing resistance.
Before I go
I look around
walls window floor
and feel an emptiness I want to leave.
What's intact I take.
To close the door
I lift the iron cat.
That comes too.

Traffic

Open the Highway Code
and there's the Lord's Prayer.
Religion apart, most people are responsible
and handle their cars tenderly.
Even in the rush-hour
traffic can be sensitive to the psychotic woman at the edge of a pavement
shouting at her voices as she waits to cross.
When we don't travel closely enough to our feelings
it's useful to remember
the mad are right about the conditions.
In her delusions she controls the traffic of our small worlds
and knows how human understanding changes by the hour
as various weathers flow through our veins.
When I shorten my sentences to record what she says,
I don't know why it is
but one of her voices
is the song of a blackbird slowed right down.
If everyone could hear it
the removal of the routine of police arresting windblown hair
would sap public confidence.
Sanity relies on our ignorance of many of the journeys we go on.
Every second is in need of us,
but were we to travel more slowly
we would catch a glimpse of the parallel dimension
where either we don't exist or we live forever.
It's here stillness fills with activity
and emotions career towards one another at different speeds
on roads that lead out of town.
At a junction
where blood runs into the chalk police use
to draw round a body after a farewell skid
seeds germinate in the tyre-marks on the soft verge.
Each stem of cow parsley in the grass there
is a shrine to commemorate the passing of life under wheels.
Whether it's a crashed van on a scrap-heap,
a vehicle abandoned in a field
or a crowded carpark where people leave their thoughts,

deep under all traffic, past and present, lurks desire.
That's why it's so good to drive to the muzak of exhausts,
to the rhythm of fumes
and to the pitch of the city's disembodied street-corner voices
of those who still look both ways before passing from one
instant to the next.
Be it the road, the engine, the gears, the clutch, the view, the
speed,
the touch of the pedal under the sole of the shoe
or the sound of a soul departing,
each moment offers the chance to worship at a luxury motel
where, as the hours purr by,
things that shouldn't be said and done go on all the time
building a crescendo of wonder from our shame.
Out of reverence to oblivion
our eyes, reflected in the dials of the dashboard, close.
And so
for those who don't believe in God,
the best way to pray is blindfold with the foot hard down on the
accelerator
knowing the brakes aren't working.

Being

Always a bunch of yellow flowers found on the path
or answers to correspondence.
Pursuit of control brings comfort
to the prison of good behaviour,
to the centre of being,
but finding the right person is accidental
and scented air is renowned for instinct.

Whatever is missing is ours
as being together is what we want from our time here.
Back through the archives
you know the things you know and how to be.
It's so easy, the new tolerance
and the places people discover.
So what a relief it is then to come out
from under what seems right
into all we have.

Violin

sweat
a headband
your tight mouth
your frown
eyes down
the bow on the strings
Beethoven's sonata no. six in A major
the last movement
I've never seen anyone put so much feeling into it
fingers at speed
flowers on your black dress
all day I've been trying
to write this
I'd love to play like you
have a freckle on my shoulder in the same place

Nocturne

From pollen in the lunar orchard
ripeness falls like silver onto lawns.
A bitten shiny fruit with crescent bruises
keeps its fist of flavour in its skin.
How cool it is and high up when I pick them
in apple hatcheries where pips are born,
pippin moons from which the whole crop spins.

Cider-making in Herefordshire

In a bad year cider is made of stones.
Blood in the apples means more deaths,
hinges are squeakier, mother has washday ribs
and the ploughman gets drunk on peelings.
The jiggery-pokery of rigor mortis
is stumped by felling and blunt pruning,
but there's no time to be upset.
When you have to get on with it
hard work is nursed through thick and thin
despite the ones the next storm takes with it.
As the poor take another bite their crisp mouths shrink
but the alcohol runs on through the century
to thirsty days of a sweeter kind.
Once all the bungling is cobbled together
and a boot is put in the mouth of the earth
a well-heeled beverage is on the way,
its fruit in harness, the body between the shanks.
Shafts of sunlight creak under each cart of ripeness
while the drunk wheel trundles on in a rough cider rut
to where the waggoner dumps his squeaky load
and leaves a short-cut silence behind him.
He hasn't much to say to the women
who fill the oxwain by the basketful.
Balancing on flimsiness, the leaves gossip
as whispers are smuggled in through the branches,
but there's not a lot of elbow-room in the crown
where the Hagloe Crab is held in high esteem.
By the time the pickers have finished their hands have vanished.
Then the trees are hit with polting lugs
and the mason smooths down the grinder
so colour is tightened and the kernel is hit.
What is batted back with a wooden spatula
lodges at the edge in these engines of pungency.
The machines look pretty. At the festival of pressing
a noisy horse makes the cogs go
jerking the teeth on the axle so the orchard is crushed
till it gets boring in leather and chains
and each nut, pip, and bolt gets a mention.

Even the moon is squeezed with a belt
so its last bit of light plops in the liquid.
Midnight excites it; its brightness escapes and shines on.
In a brewer's landscape the rind of the district,
plus core, stalks and all, change the flavour.
Every grower is known by his fruit:
Pauson, Royal Wilding, Golden Pippin, Dymmock Red.
The Stire puts a bloom on the cheeks
while the Redstreak draws from a deep strong land.
Getting the casks right is important,
the rougher workings rarely filled to the bung,
and there are several rackings before blood is added.
When a shoulder is stuck in the vat the meat dissolves
just as the odd dead rat makes the drink taste better,
and agitated fluid ferments earlier
with a rosy prospect caught in the booze.
Two hogsheads is a good day's labour
for ciderists drunk on the proceeds.
When the church bells are asunder at harvest
and worship is no longer marketable
another skinful of history's dizzy with bubbles,
the excess plonked in the font.
Though good times last longer from bottles, it's not all like this.
In a bad year cider is made out of stones.

Pat Grehan's Land

To the right and up the track between the fields
are what the locals call *The Stones*
set according to the stars,
old and cool and smooth and hard to find
unless you know Pat Grehan's Land.

Ivy

Ivy grows even while you talk
like knitting.
When it requires a new home
it is a quiet poison
that creeps without being heard
up the outside wall and in
through the window
to cover your body
and in through your open mouth
to eat you from inside
while you are sleeping.
Ivy is no fool.
It is of a wicked botany
to be found only in the dark
greens of uncertain shades.

The owl

The owl hollows his hoot out of old oak,
and when he puts on the boot of his flight
I feel so comfortable on his back.

His search for mice
is as if they were stars in his cat's-eyes.

Though his feathers ache,
he keeps his wings and feet fit with gymnastic equipment.

When the doorbell goes
it is either the milkman, the paperboy or the postman.
It will not be the owl.

Ginger Biscuit

A pair of eyes in the undergrowth.
Breathing, still warm,
the kitten we found won't move.
Attempting a rescue
I cradle distress.

We live on a tender curve,
learn to carry, to hug, to bury.
Now, before us, a tiny animal fades.
I let our daughter hold what's dead,
discover what emptiness feels like,
rest time in her palm.

Chromosomes end where I dig,
but a claw might take root,
rise like a rose.
Under the lilac,
two bits of wood nailed together,
on them our daughter writes
Ginger Biscuit. Lost.

I list different losses.
The smallest holes in the world
contain dropped coins,
missing keys, frustration.
Next comes the empty basket
home from the vet.
Moving on, I'm reminded how,
in darkness under Orion
I frequently see the constellation depict
an alternative outline,
a boy about to jump off a swing.
He's so close I want to reach out.
It's important to touch what's gone.
I remember a battery run flat
by headlights left on in a hospital carpark.
Truth has large eyes.
How they stare.

Marmaduke

Back down the path
our tortoise, slower than ever,
won't eat lettuce.
But why?
The season of food isn't over.
It's not hibernation.
Marmaduke's universe cools.
He takes his last step.
Newton's Laws of Motion are changing.
Planets stop on their orbits.
A moment congeals.
The day cracks open.

As a grown-up it's hard to cry.
I want to run to the house
to my mother and father –
but round me's
a shell I can't break out of.
The day I do
is the day I'll discover
the lakes in my eyes,
the trees and the hills they reflect,
the greater expanses,
a turtle, the world on its back.
Columbus sails another Atlantic
and dies.

La Rue du Chat Qui Pêche

What are we to name the street,
the one too dark to photograph,
the narrow one you always miss
leading down between the tall old buildings no-one lives in
to the quayside where a cat
fishes in the river?

Vanishing point

Atlantic breakers.
On the beach a girl with no legs.
France, just after the war.
Hair the colour of sand.
I wanted to look.
It's not fair.
Some things are hard to write.
When I can't find the words
it goes quiet.
Afraid of leaving her out of a poem,
I kept a clean sheet of paper aside.
Day after day it stayed blank.
At night I left the light on over it.
For years there was nothing.
Then I heard waves.
Lines of writing appeared.
Instead of punctuation
I put in footprints that should have been hers.
Today she's less than a dot on a map.
I'm not marked either,
but on a peninsula
mine's the last house,
the one at the edge of the rocks,
the first if you come by boat.
In the posts that carry the power to the end of the land
Beethoven hums.
Like verse running out
the number of cables dwindles
as the road I'd love that girl to walk down
goes on.

Absolute Zero

Most poetry readings are boring.
Most people don't bother with them.
Some poets try popping up between bands at gigs
but they're still ignored.

On the 12th March 2000
in the Independent on Sunday
the poet and critic Ruth Padel
said of the poem *No* by Mark Doty
the dominant sound in the first stanza is
the EL/EEL ending
as in feel, turtle, hall, thrill, pulled, he'll,
table, smell, candles,
leading up to the words
single shell.
I think this sort of stuff
gives poetry a bad name.
It's why poets often end up
reading to an almost empty room.
And I used to think
having no audience at all
was the worst it could get.

Nought degrees Centigrade
is the freezing point of water
but on the Kelvin scale
nought
is the point at which
subatomic particles come to rest.
In degrees Centigrade
it equals minus two seven three
and is known as Absolute Zero.

Now imagine this.
A freezing December night. Driving snow
and I turn up to give a poetry reading
at the Methodist Hall
New Holland, near Barton-on-Humber, North Lincs, DN31 7QT

It starts at eight.
Half-eight and no-one's appeared.
No. Not even the caretaker.
I'm still standing shivering outside.
What's worse than having no audience
is not being able to get into your own reading yourself.
Absolute Zero.

The World Reading

At the World Poetry Reading upstairs in Nelly's
the rule is
no-one reads a poem
written by anyone English.
The audience is largely British, white mostly,
but some asylum-seekers turn up.
One of them lights a cigarette
comes out to the front
and recites his own stuff in Kurdish.
I don't know any Kurdish.
I'm just left with the sounds,
vocal chords, breath, tongue, lips, teeth, guttural noises,
his arms going.
I know I shouldn't
but I drift off
to when I was back at primary school and they put on music
so we could all be autumn leaves
being blown about the room
and to some years later when noise became more serious
lost its music and turned into physics.
In the laboratory
to find the frequency of middle C in a tube
we had to note the distance between little piles of dust at the nodes.
I was more aware then
of the distance between myself and exams
than I was of the distance between myself and pain
or myself and excitement
but I can see now from the other Kurds here
that this poet's hit the high notes.
There's enough in what he's saying
to startle, infuriate, amaze, confuse, surprise, disgust, astound,
amuse, enrage, astonish, terrify, endear and delight.
He stops.
He stubs out his fag.
We clap.
He sits down
puts his head in his hands
and sobs.

The Ultimate Poem

I'm writing a poem.
This one's going to be truly astonishing
brilliant.
I clear the decks
shove on loads of coffee to make a start.
At last I've something important to say.
It'll really hit the big time
this one.
This one's going to have everyone laughing and weeping.
It'll make newspaper headlines.
I'll be asked to read on radio
t.v.
It'll get translated abroad
appear on university courses
get taught in schools all over the world.
For my booklaunch
fans will queue overnight.
I'll sign every flyleaf
and after shaking my hand
they won't want to wash for a week.
I no longer care about
all the stuff I've scribbled to date.
I won't have got pissed every night
on superstrength lager
for years of drunken ramblings for nothing.
The tons of scrap paper I've filched from work
will have been worth it.
This one'll show you.
Just wait till you hear it.
I'll read it out to you
when it's done.

Tenpin bowling

In my vodka-soaked cries
you can detect the noise of sizzling vegetables
and remnants of cannon-shot from the Spanish Armada.
Yes dear, you say
to try to shut me up
but I throw back my head
and open my jaws even wider.
Sound solidifies
and out of my mouth spring a snooker table
Mussolini, 5000 editions of the Daily Express
a giant ant-eater
and a signal from
Voyager II saying
the world's in cloudy beta-wave high temperature danger
and we must dance and sing our way through.
By means of natural and un-natural selection,
by means of jellyfish, coinage and furniture
we must combat those who say it's disgraceful
for Colleen to be kissed
for Man U to be thrashed by Liverpool
for the train arriving at platform nine to be smoking a pipe.
I won't be defeated.
Neither will planet earth.
We have to change what we do
and to change what we do we need to allow
Shakespeare's leopardskin handcuffs to be unlocked,
the silver Paraguayan ostrich to attend the Trooping of the
Colour
and the hot-dog primrose to flower.

Re-framing

When the name is Bob
Bob is coded
in fascinating 'High Code',
the name in Bob
as in self to me
being the names recorded.

For code under Family
I name old code 'K.G.B. Copy',
filing you
under the code called 'Too Small'.

Also in code
the proper name P. Fields,
which is Karen's
coded in a new code
known as 'Rough and Ready'
and re-named 'The Loved One'
by code-setter Bob.

Racing your own yacht

With the Stanley knife
I cut the green carpet that smells of sweaty feet, spilled beer, stale
deodorant
and the previous householder's Rottweiler, Bess.
Bits of rubber from the perished underfelt stick to my jumper
as we roll up the dirtier half and jam it in the back of the Transit ready
for the tip.
Having nothing else to go on the floor
we've left the better bit of carpet down for the moment.
From the back-bedroom where there's some black mould I can't identify
and a damp patch on the ceiling where the gutter outside's been
leaking
you point out seagulls wheeling over garden waste,
dud car batteries, scrap metal, paper recycling bins and the bottlebank
at the Corporation's reprocessing plant where we're about to go.
Moving's always a bit of a bind, but thank God the worst of it's over
and I've remembered to fetch in the spring that fell in the puddle from
the Parker Knoll chair
when you took it up the back alley past the new neighbour's kids
who'd just buried Cindy the ladybird and put a pebble on her grave.
Oh, and that's another thing,
once it's been to the launderette, that elasticated ironing-board cover
you rescued from the slurry outside the back door
should brighten up the living-room a bit.
It's a pity the drain in the yard's blocked.
Though I'm left-handed, that right-handed yellow rubber glove
discarded on the street
will come in handy when using the beer can to ladle out the rest of the
gravel, plastic clothes pegs and worms.
Once most of the sludge is out
and we've waggled an unwound wire coat-hanger around in the
narrow aperture at the bottom
there's nothing a bit of caustic or concentrated sulphuric acid won't
shift,
especially if you ignore the instructions and pour in the whole lot
undiluted first
taking care to jump back as you tip a bucket of boiling water on top.
Till then we'll just have to empty the washing-up water down the loo.
Pinching my fingers unloading the bookcase
shows we should never be without a first aid kit.
The trouble is the elastoplast was in one of the bin-liners at the back of
the van at the time

and I couldn't find the scissors.
I'm so glad we got here from the old place we could no longer afford
the rent on.
I never thought we'd get that fire surround round the banisters
and down through the door at the bottom of the stairs without you
doing your back in again.
In the long run the small mortgage we have now will give us a bit of
security for our old age.
If only I knew someone with an electric cooker well enough
I could ask them if they'd mind you coming round with the Phillips
screwdriver you've temporarily mislaid
to undo their junction box so you can see where the green flex of the
earth on ours should go.
In the meantime we've had to abandon this week's mutton stew in
favour of cheese biscuits and lemon curd.
So far I've picked up thirty-nine p in small change from the landing and
the hall
and there's loads of hairpins we'll have to watch out for when
hoovering.
By the way, did you know the vacuum's on the blink?
Never mind,
there's a super fashion docu-soap on the box tonight about life on the
catwalk
followed by another programme called *Racing Your Own Yacht*.

And now here's another

It's called MacDonald's Guide to the Emotions.
I more or less copied it straight out of Merlin's
Ninety-Seven Premier League Official Sticker Collection
keeping my recent encounter with someone called Barbara in
mind as I did so.
There's a bit in it where she squeezes me in a carpark
sending testosterone down the MI to my groin.
Later on she touches my arm.
We collide at junction twenty six
and stay together but I'm thinking
this can't really be love and I do all the grief stuff internally in
advance
so that by the time she turns me off by turning off at the next
slip road
to announce she only wants to stay good friends
I'm able to swing across a huge spectrum of previously worked
through feelings
in three seconds flat.
After that I go on metaphorically
about my various states of mind
and those of others such as Barbara
in relation to a whole load of A roads with numbers after them
followed by masses of map references.
In essence, what I seem to be trying to say in this piece
is how, in the interests of self protection,
it's important to retain a smidgen of cynicism
provided,
whether you're alone or with someone else,
it doesn't stop you
getting off the main highway once in a while
and onto the skinny tracks
that peter out into the wonderful mountains
we're well advised to make molehills of
if we're not to end up in tears at the office the next day.

That's about it really.

Band-Aid

There was a young woman called Prendergast
Who spent hours in search of elastoplast
It must have been three
When she bandaged her knee
Though I think it could have been twenty past.

Limerick

There was a young man from Kingston upon Hull
who couldn't write limericks to save his life.
He'd no sense of rhythm
and the rhyme was non-existent
so he gave up.

Making sense of the world

Till I couldn't get into the match
I thought I knew the difference between a football and a ticket.
Before a member of the allotment committee arrived in time
for the meeting on the purchase of seed potatoes despite a flat
tyre
I was able to distinguish between puncture and punctuality.
I didn't believe there was a connection between the
Elizabethan Reformation and a tin of dog-food,
then, in the middle of a t.v. documentary on English history,
up popped an advert for Pedigree Chum.
Sometimes I think I make sense of the world,
that I'm certain I can tell brake fluid from wine
only to hear someone who was driving over the limit
blame his motorway accident on the mechanic who serviced
his car.
You might say Europe and a knitting needle are in no way
related,
but what about the demand in Switzerland by skiers for woolly
jumpers
and how the pattern of footwork on a ballroom floor
establishes a similarity between a Japanese dancing girl and
the earth's crust?
A plume of smoke and a nesting puffin present no problem
as soon as the letter 'g' is added to the bird's name.
Okay, how about a blood transfusion and a flat-bottomed
boat?
Both concern vessels.
There's no end to this carry-on.
It's the alchemy the intellect applies to crosswords as it tries to
turn base metals into clues.
I'm no longer sure I'd know a stick of gelignite from a
nightingale
now I have my fingers in my ears.

P.J.S.

The first anyone knew anything was wrong with him
was when another boy
accidentally sat on his hand
on one of the benches in the dining hall
and broke his wrist.
When he came back the next term
he'd had a leg taken off –
the wooden one they fitted
didn't bend at the knee.
I can see him now in our school sanatorium.
I'd had to go up there with a nosebleed
after a collision on the rugby pitch.
The nurse told me
he wasn't very well.
He was too weak to get up to see the temperature chart at the end of his bed.
When I looked at it for him
it was like a mountain range
but I said it was okay.
The school was on the Lancashire coast
and we used to be made to go out running along the sea wall in all weathers.
They said it toughened us up.
I can still feel the spray stinging my face from the breakers
bashing against the concrete promenade.
Sometimes I used to think I'd never get back for afternoon lessons –
that I always did came as a bit of a surprise
because I was no good at games and thought of myself as weak.
I was one of the lucky ones.
He wasn't.
As he lay there he told me
when he grew up
he was going to direct films
but a day or two later he died.
In a different universe
chance takes us another way
which makes me wonder whether I really did write all those novels
I said I would
and what his contribution to the cinema has been.

Charlie

He took us for French
Charlie Dale.
He'd been a prisoner of war.
Beaten and whipped
the kids said.
In lessons
he used to sling his chair round the room.
He'd scream.
He'd laugh.
He'd leap up to water his plants.
He'd shout.
But you never knew when.
If you could
you sat at the back.
You kept your head down.
The words burned
and you hoped the ones that mattered
the ones on which you were going to be tested
stuck.

In that class
a boy called Jenkins
always came bottom
yet Jenkins sat at the front
and Charlie would humour Jenkins.
I don't know why.

Then Smithson turned up
and Charlie humoured him too.
Because of his course of treatment
Smithson was often late.
The previous term
he'd lost a leg.
No-one said
but I think we knew
it was cancer.
The lives of others.
We know so little really
don't we?

How what and why
are largely unanswered.

Though I passed the exam
I've forgotten the French
but I do remember the chair
the wooden one Charlie slung round the room.
Its legs scraped and clattered across the boards.
The back smacked the wall.
It made me jump.
I can hear it now.

Garden

A child's bike upside down on a lawn.
The door of an empty summerhouse open.
A handbasin
complete with taps
in the nettles.
Holes in the leaves of cherry, field maple and ash.
A ladybird searching for aphids on a twig.
Rusty mould on a dockleaf.
Crab-apple branches sag with ripeness.
Drops of water gleam on the grass
where on a rotten plum
a red admiral folds and unfolds its wings.
I hear the relentless hum of distant traffic.
A jet zooms over.
I see a flock of small birds
rise from the trees.
I make the best of these things while they last
as time flies away at the speed of light.
Each moment's barely a couple of seconds.
One day I won't be here.

Tom

In the Edinburgh shelter for drunks
who found it too cold to sleep rough
I'd steer clear of Tom.
When he was pissed
his bald head shone,
a warning, if you got too close
he'd butt you and bust your nose,
a true 'Glasgow kiss'.
When it was time to doss down
everyone called for Tom. We loved his party trick.
He'd stand on the camp beds
and, one by one, bare-handed,
take out the lit bulbs.
His polished dome gleamed in the dark.

Nineteen eighty-six. East Germany. Power in short supply.
At night from the train, the odd glimmer,
a village, a farm.
The city of Magdeburg passed.
I didn't even see it.
The darkness made me think of Tom's party trick,
Tom's bid for power,
about what takes the light out of our lives.

In the new place the grill on the cooker is a bit fierce

Some amazing reductions in the IKEA sale
and in the world of science.
On a scale a millionth the size of an atom
time goes backwards.
July the second moves about aimlessly
and much as I'd expect
Richard the Third
is on at a cinema near me.
The river I follow
meanders like a swan's neck.
Floating downstream
a plank turns in the current.
I can go anywhere, be anything,
do what I want.

Back home on a sheet of scrap I use for this poem
someone's pencilled a message for Pam to phone Lisa at work.
Who knows what'll happen next?
If tomorrow ever comes
kippers for breakfast will stink the house out
and now the car's got through its M.O.T.
I can afford a new chair.

Empty chair

The therapist tells me
to imagine I'm two people
and to talk to my other half
on the empty chair opposite.

But I don't like that chair
I tell her
and we spend hours
arguing over this

till eventually
she lets me
bring in my favourite one
from the next room.

The black chair

On Friday I bought the black chair you wanted so much.
I got it for four pounds down because of its loose legs
but I thought it would be o.k. for me to sit in and
think for a few years.

When I got it home, we tried it in various parts of the room
to see where it would best fit.
You wanted a geranium beside it and I didn't like it
near the window.

Then you said you wanted to write music on the wall,
a shower of minims and crotchets in the corner
where we had finally decided the chair should stand.

Although what I had paid for the chair had put us further into debt,
the current economic climate was sufficiently favourable
for the banks to lend money.

The only remaining problem would be
convincing them I was a good investment sitting there
reading and thinking,
and reading, and thinking again.

English Lit

The A level English Lit paper.
I'm really sweating to remember
who said what in Act Three Scene One
of Romeo and Juliet.
The sun shines into the hall.
The invigilator paces up and down.
Twenty minutes to go
and I've only done two sides.
I'll be lucky if I get a pass.
Shakespeare's in the next row.
He's doing the same exam on his own play.
He looks at the trees outside the window and scratches his head.
I take a peek over his shoulder.
He's written even less than me.

William and Francis

A touring Shakespeare troupe hits town.
The theatre agent rings us.
One of the actors wants B & B.
He's playing Romeo.

After the first night
Romeo comes back late.
He turns the key in our door.
Juliet sneaks in behind him.
The stairs creak.
His bed creaks.
Come the morning
Juliet's gone.

At breakfast, over eggs and fried bread,
Romeo tells us
Shakespeare didn't write Shakespeare
Bacon did.

Brilliant sky

To hit hard
I used to think
poetry had to have
tragedy angst and pain.
David was my brother
and killed himself
is how Diane Wakoski
starts her poem
Some Brilliant Sky.

For years I tried to write like that
and wrote about
a friend whose boy
got eighteen months for sleeping with his sister,
a neighbour's cancer,
my two divorces,
how at school I stole a mole trap,
at thirty nine
got done for drunken driving,
how a distant cousin
had a child by someone else before he married.
I even drowned my father.
Then I shot him
and gassed my mother
twice.

They say the sky's the limit. For me it was
and brilliant too.

Blood terror fear shame theft
sex fangs death guns.
I had to get it down.
Then one day in the kitchen
I was peeling spuds.
Diane Wakoski was on the radio
talking about her brother
and how she got pestered after readings.
Letters. Phonecalls.

How and why
he stood at the edge of the cliff and jumped.
In the end
she'd had to tell
her listeners and her readers
she'd never had a brother.
She'd lied.

The gas man

the doorbell
the doorbell
the gas man
the gas man
I let him in
I let him in
I let him into the poem as well
he's come to read the metre

At the Cavendish

In the Cavendish Research Laboratory canteen
the astrophysicists are doing a Highland Reel.
The automatic drink dispenser’s on the blink
but never mind, they can use the bar.
The universe has just flung its kilt in the air
so the radio telescope can have a quick feel
and find another star.

Page 138

Turn aside from dehydration to graceful deformity
from offers of a break in the two-thirty at Sedgefield Park
to the breath-taking dawn of a foggy foggy day

drugs and the mooing of cattle apart,
take up Gaelic
and sign on for a weekend workshop
in how to make ear-rings from corrugated iron

I tell you
too much accuracy makes the populace incandescent

how do I know this?
I don't
I made it up
just as I do when I say growing a beard's exhausting
or the group sex industry's really taken off.
bla di bla di bla
at which point six people get up and walk out
just as the milk's going off
and the mischievous ivy
reaches the top of the lovesick balustrade

Approaching Kongsberg

low cloud
the tops of spruce behind tall birches
flashes of sunlight
buds swelling
melting ice at a river's edge
hydro-electric power
the shadow of the train's pantograph on a passing rockface
a tunnel
then mountains reflected in a fjord
and the train speeding up
a tractor-powered sawbench
a man in overalls bending over a heap of logs
his back to us
how life is
much of it watched
some unlived but not missed
a need to feel sad?
no not sad
and finding the right way to say just that

> she discharged herself from hospital
> and was found on the kitchen floor the next morning

the train slowing again now
you next to me doing a crossword
the letter before s turns out to be an e
our carriage tilting slightly
a frozen lake
www dot nsb dot no
Norway State Railway
and me looking for the right word for saplings in a clearing
tree-less snow-capped peaks in the distance
our tickets are punched
we don't need our reserved seats
enough space for a better view from ones by the window

they got her up out of bed
she wanted to look inland
see across the roofs of the town before she died

over the top of the glasses I need for reading
more hills
and nearer the track a house with some sheds
a sudden hollow sound from the wheels
as we cross a bridge over a road

For all we know

I'm in the cab
of the white Mercedes truck
John's driving.

On Radio Four
Billie Holliday sings
For All We Know
recorded in 1947
near the end of her life.

We're going through the flatter
blanker greener bits
of the East Riding
delivering photocopying paper.

It's 1.46pm tenth of Feb. 2002.
A light wind. Cloudy. Sunny intervals.
11 degrees Celsius.

The next drop
6 boxes of A4
is at Imprint
Unit 16
on the industrial estate
outside Market Weighton.

Ex-Tory Chancellor of the Exchequer
Ken Clark
is hosting the programme.
No doubt he's wearing his Hush-Puppies
and baggy suit.

In our grubby jeans and trainers
John and I agree
despite his politics
we like the guy.
We'd feel easy with him
if he were with us now.

John pulls up,
backs the truck
into the printer's yard
surrounded by
Cupressus Leylandii.

He won't need help with this lot
so I pick up my book
from the dash-board shelf
and from the detailed account
of Nazi-occupied Europe
learn how a German commander
gave some country lads
a reading test
in a farm-yard.
The ones who could read
were put in the group
who thought they were going to be clerks.

But because people who could read
were dangerous
they were shot.

Here in the cab
the tachograph whirrs.
I'm 59.
The world's fighting terrorism.

The delivery done
John climbs back in
with the invoice.

I close the book.
For a second
my mind goes back
to how
at the age of 11
Billie Holliday was raped
by the neighbour
of her mother's
lover.

She's on her last song.
Ken Clark
closes the programme.
John starts the engine
puts the truck in gear
and drives off.

Walking

I haven't seen you for ages.
You've a beard now
grey bushy hair
hiding that schoolboy face
and I'm sitting beside you again
and we're helping each other out like we used to
with the papers and forms.
There's a task to be done
but now
there are two sticks by your seat
to help you walk
and I don't say anything.
My eyes glance off a screen
I steer round
go over and under
rather than through
and though we're beside each other
I'm beside myself
with shyness
or could it be
anger
            fear
                        or rage
and if it is
what might that be about
those two sticks of yours
these legs of mine.

Home visit

The mother's just called me in over their daughter.
The mother, the daughter and I
sit in the front room.

A crash upstairs.
It's the father
flinging the dressing-table drawer
against the bedroom wall.

We freeze.

That's him waking up after being at the pub.

We hear him come down
his brick shit-house body suddenly filling the doorway.

He staggers towards me.
I stand up.
I'm a social worker I say.
I shake his hand.
I sit down.

He towers above me
sweaty and shouting
one hand on each arm of my chair
his red face inches from mine.

The daughter's crying.
The mother tells him
she rang and asked me to come.
He spins round
and sends her flying.
Her head hits the skirting.
Blood spatters the wall.

Still in my chair
I'm shaking.
Screaming, the daughter dashes out into the street.

How does it finish?
It doesn't,
things like this don't.
If I hadn't gone
it wouldn't have happened
but I did
and it did.

These things do.

Ready and waiting

One of the playground jokes
was if anyone was daft or different or mad
men in white coats
would come and cart them off
to the loony bin in a green van.
If you couldn't play the violin well
the best way to stop being bullied
was not to play it at all.
Not to be picked on
you'd keep your toes
more or less straight to the front
when you walked.

Going to school
we sometimes saw Johnny.
Meningitis at 14
had left him
not right in the head.
He looked barely 20.
In fact he was 40
and kicked out his feet at 10 to 2 when he walked.
His mother was dead.
An only child
he lived with his father.
With Johnny
genealogy stopped.

We didn't care.
Here was some extra-terrestrial bait.
We'd run up shouting
and point and laugh
and shove him around.
He'd lash out.
We'd dive out the way.
But we sometimes got hit.
It was like a bullfight
with Johnny as bull.
For us it was better than cowboys and Indians

or soccer or climbing trees.
The green van's coming, we'd shout.
Though my father and his
went shooting together
for target practice on Sundays
my parents never found out
the torment I caused.
Johnny hadn't the nous
to tell tales.

Sometimes I'd see him in his front room
playing the violin
to stray battered tomcats.
You'd see them lined up at the window
till an alarm clock he'd set
went off.
Ours was a middle class street
where people vacuumed their carpets
but when his father got cancer
and the doctor was coming
they said
Johnny cleaned out the room
with a yard brush.
After the funeral
Johnny lived on alone in the house for a while
and one day the chimney caught fire.
We knocked the knocker to tell him.
When he opened the door
smoke drifted past us.
He'd pissed his pants.
Inside
the room was hot
and bits of red-hot brick
fell into the grate.
I don't remember what we did next
but a fire engine came.

This is a story of fire and death and the violin.
It's a story of time alarm and urine
meningitis and cancer.

It’s not in the lists of best sellers.
In fact it’s right off the scale
like playing a fiddle above the bridge till it squeals.
It’s a story of ammunition and war.
As I say
the room had been hot.
What we didn’t know then
was the risk to our eyes our feet our hands
from the cartridges for his father’s rifle
in a cupboard next to the fireplace.

Fire

You should have seen it.
The smoke. The flames.
Red-hot brick. Charcoal.
Exploding glass.
The picture on the front page.
The headlines.
It was our school.
Brigades from the region.
Twelve engines. Five tenders.
Hoses and ladders.

All the classes were out watching.
We should have been doing physics
but we'd found a new way of understanding heat.

Whenever I think about it
it still warms me
to hear that cheer go up
every time the roof falls in.

Each time the fire's put out
after the steam and damping down
the unburned world returns
and though the glass is back in the windows
and the Phoenix has been restored to the classics
the questions of my own burning still remain –
what fire means
and when the ash has cooled and blown away
what stays.

Woodyard

Behind me
elms slide to and fro on a trolley
as they're sliced for coffins.
Jim stacks the boards in the yard.
I'm in a corner on off-cuts.
Next to me
Bill points motorway fence posts.
The scream that follows the first bite of metal in wood
turns into a whine.
At every machine
each tree's a song.
It's before the Health and Safety at Work Act.
There aren't any ear-muffs or masks.
Through muscle and risk on a minimal wage
a hand can stray from a wandering mind
to high speed teeth.
The benches don't have guards.
Some of the men are deaf.
Bill's mouth moves,
I mouth a reply.
The tea-break's the first time you stop.
When a band-saw hits a nail in a trunk
it snaps and shoots off.
Holes in the roof are proof.
As a sharp reminder
a blade's been known
to wing its way sideways across the shop floor instead.

Evaluation

On the stage
people with learning disabilities
sit silently by xylophones and drums.
A woman with thin grey hair holds a tambourine.
We've come to the Louth Literature Festival
where, in accordance with the council's policy of inclusion,
their performance is to open the event.

I feel awkward
our having to walk to the front
to take the only two seats left.
We pick up the programmes and evaluation sheets on our chairs
and sit down.

The percussion begins.
A girl stutters into a mike
reciting words I can't make out.
Two boys
are carrying a life-size papier-maché baby elephant
towards us.
One of them manipulates the trunk
now only inches from my nose
as a trombone blasts.
Dressed as a monkey
one of the carers struts about
to the beat.

The piece ends.
The audience clap
and after winning poems and stories
by members of the general public
have been read out to more applause
we fill in our evaluation sheets
on which we're also asked to indicate
who we are.

I tick the boxes that describe me.
50-65.
White.
Male.

Things to make and do

electroplating children
    a battery operated switchback for breasts and testicles
how to install a burglar alarm on a seesaw
    erecting a corner cupboard in a steeple
how to pick up a folding cat
    a machine for talking to pigeons
  cleaning and adjusting a wire-haired fox terrier
    suggestions for laying out a dead gramophone
how to put a skylight in a pair of jeans
    a pouch to keep doors and windows in
how to improve France
how to sink a well in a hearthrug
    care and control of unstable underpants
    tips on wrestling with a three-tier lightning conductor
    safety first in poetry

Black Beauty

Flowers flown in from Jersey.
It's the best you can do.
My stomach's the size of a walnut.
Wires plugged into the mains keep me going.
The current's enough to shock an eel.

Above my bed
the ceiling clears
and I'm looking into the pond that filled our childhood.
On its surface
tiny
scuttling
waterboatmen
and us with jamjars
poised at the edge.

By the way
thanks for the card.
Were you able to splash best wishes
they'd cool me.

Remember how we used to sit quiet on the bank by my house
and wait for rabbits?
Though I've almost run out of notions of mother and father
the garden's returning in fragments.
Suddenly everything in it
rises out of the vase on my bedside locker
filling the hospital ward
with one huge spray of delight.

Wayback
my mother read me a book called Black Beauty,
the name of a horse.
Here, they're pumping Black Beauty into my veins.
I'd love you to feel the stampede.
As blood turns to air
I see you beside me.
From now on we can be horses.
We'll charge across fields
jumping fences and hedges,
our manes to the wind.
And the fun we'll have on the hills!

What it all boils down to

What it all boils down to
is this

Other poetry from Ragged Raven Press:

People from bones by Bron Bateman and Kelly Pilgrim (2002)
£6.50 ISBN 0 9542397 0 9
This is a beautiful book which I very much enjoyed reading and I can recommend to anyone who loves poetry. **Jenny Hamlett, Poetry Monthly**
The work of two poets who tackle life with wit and sympathy ...Together they have created an excellent collection and deserve a wide audience. **New Hope International**

the cook's wedding by John Robinson (2001)
£6.99 ISBN 0 9520807 8 8
I especially like the vim, the large-heartedness, the celebration of life and locality. **U. A. Fanthorpe**
Accessible, visual and rich. **The New Writer**

Saturday Night Desperate (anthology 2003) £6) ISBN 0 9542397 2 5
A whole host of good things...emphasising the excellence of contemporary poetry today...You'll read it time and again. **Bluechrome**

The promise of rest (anthology 2002) £6 ISBN 0 9520807 9 6
This is one of those anthologies where you don't look for what's good, but what is exceptional ... an excellent collection. **Purple Patch**
An intriguing showcase of real life stills and vignettes in a sparkling variety of mood, colourful imagery and colloquially attuned word and phrase. **Voice and Verse**
One of my favourite presses. **Abi Hughes-Edwards, The New Writer**
Ragged Raven are fast gaining a reputation as serious, committed publishers of quality contemporary poetry. **Raw Edge**

Red Hot Fiesta (anthology 2001) £6 ISBN 0 9520807 7 X
Strong, tight and characterful. **New Hope International**

Smile the weird joy (anthology 2000) £6 ISBN 0 9529897 6 1
An overflowing cornucopia of all that is best in contemporary poetry... there is delight on every page. **Poetry Monthly**

Old songs getting younger (anthology 1999) £6 ISBN 09520807 5 3
Brings together an interesting mix of writers. **Connections**